Supernatural Science:

How to become a Great Magickian
without Losing Your Mind.

Essay about the occult No.1

By NickDutch
Graduate of Sociology and Psychology,
Student of Neuroscience and Natural Science,
Part Qualified Accountant and
Small Business Owner

ALSO:
Tarot / Divination Professional, Medium,
Practical Occultist / Magickian and Healer.

In accordance with the law of the land, this work
is to be regarded as for entertainment purposes only.
However it should be pointed out that
NickDutch takes his work and views very seriously indeed.

http://www.nickdutch.co.uk   http://www.bespoke-group.com/freelance/

Copyright year: 2008

Copyright notice: by Nick Dutch, All rights reserved

The above information forms this copyright notice : © 2008 Nick Dutch, All rights reserved.

ISBN: 978-0-9558551-0-8

Foreword.

"Magick is the Art and Science of change in Accordance with the will"
– Alister Crowley

"Magick is the art and science of changes in consciousness in accordance with the will"
– Dion Fortune

"Magick is a system of tools to change achievable reality"
– Phil Hine

"Unless the word Magick is used properly, namely to describe something which is separate to normality, and therefore only the supernatural or paranormal, and, to a certain degree within the bounds of what the common man understands by the word Magic or Magick, the word looses significance or any meaning and practitioners of magick are derided as lunatics and losers.
Magic in this supernatural context, whether it is spelled with a letter C or CK at the end must therefore be used solely for the attempt to generate supernatural activity in accordance with the will, to attempt to be miraculous and to defy:

1. the Newtonian concept of the laws of physics
2. the concepts of the soul and mind that are inherent to psychology and neuroscience
3. the laws of communication at a distance that are, in the present day restricted to telecommunication devices.
4. the understood laws about the means of gaining information that is in the present era restricted to "cold" (or fraudulent) readings, people watching, kinesthetics and the like
5. the accepted physical laws pertaining to time and space

...and to do so in a way that is realistic, without falling prey to delusion.
In the complete absence of any scientific laboratory that is sufficiently equipped, has the funding or the inclination to provide complete, in depth and serious research as to how supernatural activity can occur, we are restricted to passing on anecdotes, stories pertaining to occasional occurrences, plus some basic guides as to how an individual created, or seemed to create, certain effects and then to allow each individual to experiment and think for themselves. However the human organism is not well equipped to deal with intellectual thought, complex or seemingly different or difficult concepts, and as such many individuals are scared off studying the supernatural. A certain degree of skepticism is needed to allow the human organism to place his or her experiences into perspective, a certain degree of disbelief that can be turned on and turned off at will is required. This requires practice.
Most humans be they believers in the skeptics creed or occult "believers", seem to be prone to the disease of holding on firmly and tightly to world views rather than to be able to have some self doubt and criticism.
It is now time to lay this state of mind aside and go forward and experiment with pleasure and pride and to attempt to use your developing knowledge of how an important aspect of the natural world (you) can interact with the mundane and the seemingly Divine in ways in which you had not previously thought possible.
It is a shame that many are scared off the experimentation with the supernatural as, desired results or none, there can be nothing truly more thrilling and pleasurable as a good scare caused by an unknown and unknowable force, or a divine state of spiritual ecstasy."

– Nick Dutch

Supernatural Science.
How to become a Great Magician without losing your mind.

Without the shadow of a doubt, whether skeptics exist or argue in circles or whether they just attack you for what you are curious about, there are certain facts about the ways of the workings of the world that remain "slightly outside of our knowledge" and as such have a terrific pull on the minds of the science fiction writers and the screen writers of our ages.

Nevertheless, there is often some truth when there is some fiction, but precisely what that is, where the truth lies remains a mystery to most people (apart from of course those who are daft enough to believe that science fiction as fact and memory fragments of past lives of humans on other planets...LOL, as when a believer believes, everything is explained to the believer, without the need for intellectual thought to impose upon the beauty of the simplistic world view defined by the belief structure)

The very vague and amorphous nature of supernatural phenomena, without a laboratory suitably equipped to be able to measure, qualify and quantify certain phenomena makes it even easier for humans to make the lives of other humans a mystery through imposing mysterious and terrifying superstitious interpretations of the forces of nature on the minds of people both vulnerable and seemingly invincible. This is the mode of psychological leverage of religions, cults and the like, be they alternative or orthodox.

This is a damned shame as there is a great deal of fun to be had through generally mucking about with supernatural energy, and so far the world has been left in a vacuum of knowledge about the way that certain supernatural phenomena can be created. I would even go so far as to say that maybe 95% of all the writings about the new age or occult are useless and misinformation rather than anything that can be useful to anyone.

I had anticipated that later in life when I had become too old to be considered a threat to the orthodox community, my employer and the like, I should write about the supernatural, but as I have focused my life on being a professional commercial occult entertainer, there seems like no time like the present to do this work. I propose to criticize a lot of BS that has been written about magick, the occult and such things and then to be able to add, and create, a suitable system of occult components, so to speak, for the average person to be able to adapt to their own methodologies.

Let us start from the top, there is no such thing as an "actual technique" to perform any act of clairvoyance, telepathy and precognition, one does not need to stare at a crystal ball with only two candles either side of it and then to say special words to make the clouds vanish, one does not need to have any particular faith or religion. One does not have to read the Lords Prayer backwards. One does not need to be a devout anything apart from curious, intelligent, creative in thought, good at extrapolation, with the ability to criticize ones own thoughts and beliefs, to have the ability to assess which factors created the effect and which did not.

Funnily enough, I have spent much of my youth and life involved in the supernatural world, I have been in two witchcraft covens, have been a probationer member of the national federation of spiritual healers and have read Tarot for nearly 20 years and am now a working associate member of a professional ghost hunting group. My supernatural CV is actually longer and larger than my graduate, post graduate, work and business CV, let alone longer than the businesses that I used to run in recruitment and artwork.

What I am hoping to achieve here in this work is a collection of some my experience and knowledge that will hopefully be of either benefit or use to you the reader. I feel that it would be prudent of me to not give you any promises. If you are reading this essay to, for instance, find a way of "magicking" yourself out of debt or to find the cure to the mystery disease that you are suffering from, then I will be honest and say that you won't find that here at all. I am not going to suggest for a moment that the occult world would give you the benefits spoken of in myths, science fiction, dungeons and dragons games or in ancient grimoires or the like, and I am certainly not going to say that what you will experience though divination will give you any 100% accurate insights into national lottery numbers.

Nor am I here to convince you that it is worth while considering that psychic ability, or professional psychics are 100% trustworthy. If I did so, it would infer that you must trust all psychics, which you should not! I am genuinely appalled that much of the occult world is about creating superstitious fear, placing otherwise intelligent humans in a position of being made psychologically or financially powerless, often for political reasons or to satisfy the sick and twisted desires of certain individuals. What I will say, however is that experimenting with astral projection, ritual magick, divination, conversations with angels and spirits and other fun toys that have been given to us by nature can be the most lively, beautiful and sometimes terrifying experience of your life. It can encourage you to contemplate the meaning of human existence more and more, and to ascertain for yourself whether your consciousness is a real immortal force or an illusion created by the activity of certain brain cells. Arguably, the most important thing that I can give you is a structure for experimenting with the way that the world works.

Unfortunately for the average human being, to be able to live, you must be able to think for yourself, something that has been curtailed by teachers, scientists, bosses, politicians and church leaders for centuries, but which I believe, is your individual and immortal right. I am not saying this to attempt to dissuade you from obeying the law and I am certainly not asking anyone to engage in any revolutionary activity! But a basic background in how to think scientifically will be vital as you learn to challenge and disbelieve your own experiences.

"Why should I challenge and disbelieve my own experiences when my upbringing has taught me to believe in myself?" but if believing in yourself leads to making mistakes that you will then suffer from in later life, surely you need some self criticism? "well sure, but what the hell does that have to do with the supernatural?" the problem of the supernatural is that it is a world that is dogged and beset with believers who have various models of the world, understandings of spirits that, due to the dis-ease of belief, have become in their own minds a strange combination of theology and a reality, a concrete and un-shifting model of the way that the world works and any trespassers against their beliefs will be attacked, threatened and even worse. But not by any supernatural being, but just by believers in a cosmology or world view, namely other humans. The religious and spiritual world is more political than it may seem, and fear is the main means whereby occult and religious groups prevent any freedom of its members at all.

Just by illustration, suppose that you weren't the person that you are, but you were Charles Darwin, or maybe Einstein, Pasteur or any of the other great experimenters and thinkers of your time. And you discovered something that criticized the way that the world works. You would go though hell just as they did. But on a more subtle way, if you get involved in the supernatural and start to make some curious discoveries about the way that the world works, then you will also be liable to criticism, but more from other believers in the supernatural than by the scientists or skeptics (who would probably just see you as a lunatic anyway). But what if you were actually wrong? If you were a "proper" scientist, you would need to be able to prove your theories to the other members of the scientific community. However, as a supernaturalist you will probably want to keep your ideas purely to yourself, and that can be as dangerous to your mental health as being assaulted by skeptics. You may avoid going out at certain phases of the moon, you may have many sleepless nights as you lay awake afraid that a spiritual force will attack you when like as not, it won't. You might say something that you regret to the boss under the mistaken belief that you can then undo the damage through controlling his mind when you probably can't. In short, you need to be a rational objective scientific thinker before you can even contemplate playing with the occult.

As you experiment more and more, after a period of time, you will start to jump to conclusions, and that is a good thing, as extrapolations from some evidence can be a good thing, but the danger lies if those extrapolations get out of control, you start to believe in them, you seek out more and more evidence that you are right and others are wrong. You redo the experiment more and more and even though you have made 100 attempts that have proven you to be wrong, you seek out the one moment that proves that you are right. A very human trait, but very undesirable. What you may have failed to do here is to ascertain as a result of reasoning and education, scientific thinking applied to the supernatural, which forces or factors wee important, which ones helped, which hindered and then to ascertain what was right and what was wrong. Essentially how to proceed with experimentation.

Now, the next thing that you may or may not be thinking is why the hell is Nick using the word science when he is writing about the supernatural? Aren't these terms contradictory?

I guess not when you use the term science in its proper sense of the word. Scientists don't prove anything at all. Science does not turn the world into a world of absolute certainties at all. In fact, science does not and cannot prove anything absolutely. Science just demonstrates what is most likely to be true under specific and measurable circumstances, and then following that, there is nothing but beliefs, theories and the like, incorrectly (in terms of the usage of the English language) called a "body of knowledge".

So what is science? Simply a method for the investigation into nature. So, what can stop me from using scientific methodology when approaching the world of the supernatural? Belief in any model of the universe. If, for instance you are a Christian, and you start to sense comforting messages coming from above you when in prayer, the model of the universe will stipulate that you are experiencing the presence of God or the Words of Jesus, but in reality, all that has happened is that you have had an experience, nothing more and nothing less, just an experience. In actuality, there is no proof or evidence that the words and messages and sense of comfort is coming from God, Jesus, the Devil, Odin or some kind of other spirit entity present where you are, or indeed telepathic contact from an alien in outer space, or maybe it was just telepathy from next doors dog anyway..... Yes I know I am being frivolous now, but you need to be able to laugh at your own pompous misinterpretations of the world to try and see these experiences in perspective.

They are just experiences thats all, nothing more. The precise cause or method of delivery of these forces that precipitate these experiences are unknown, unknowable and a complete mystery, but the more that we play around with supernatural experiences, the more that we can begin to learn that under certain strange and unusual circumstances (that we can get to learn about and know at a later stage in detail through research and experimentation), strange things happen. Without the self criticism AFTER the event, we will start believing stupid ideas like our cat didn't run away, he has been taken up in the Ascentar Space Ship where the Lord will change his DNA and make our cat the next messiah.... and equally strange insanities.

"But Nick, surely you must believe in what you do?" Why? If a scientist does an experiment, does he do it to prove that his pet theory is correct? No, he does it to investigate the way that the world works, neither believing nor disbelieving in what he does. When I attempt a supernatural activity, such as a spiritual healing, when I am dong the actual activity, I choose to believe 100% that I am channeling the energy of healing down my arms and into the subject, but after the event I become the worlds most agnostic atheist skeptic and carry on doing my normal and day to day things (dealing with the bank, going shopping etc.) and I don't think of anything supernatural at all. If however my subject after the event reports that they felt electricity and heat emanating from my hands and that her bad back got tremendously improved after the healing, then we can have a pause for reflection. All I have done is to perform certain exercises in a certain way to try and get some specific results, but I had no knowledge that I would actually receive those results at all. I certainly could not state at all what forces were involved or the rules of the "higher spheres of the universe" with any certainty. And yes, situations will arise that will be completely devoid of result at all, no heat, no sense of electricity and the like. Those are the situations that I can learn from experimentally.

But the thing is to be able to learn how to turn belief on and off at will (a skill in its own right that you will need to practice with), neither to defend beliefs nor to criticize them. Now despite the fact that I have used to word "science" in this title, I am not suggesting that there are any dead cert formulas for how one can levitate, cure cancer and the like, but I can show you how to experiment and how not to go completely dooaly in the process.

Another problem with the writings on the supernatural, magick and the like is that they use words in a rather peculiar way, over simplified and downright daft. The most common phrase used by occultists is "It Works" (whether this is talking about prayer or occult techniques). Now there are many reasons why that phrase is just plain daft. Firstly it is just two words, and no phrase in just two words can be any use to anyone. It is unintelligent and demonstrates un-intelligence in anyone who uses it. Secondly the users of this phrase have not been specific, they have not broken the phenomena down into its constituent parts, in short they have not stated WHAT works, and what they mean by the phrase. Now my reading lamp that I am using to illuminate this keyboard does work, it is in working order, EVERY time I press the button on the base, thus completing the circuit, the electricity that is generated at the Central electricity generating board is pumped though the system at the correct frequency amplitude, voltage and all that jazz, and the component that emanates the light, the halogen bulb, gives off light and a bit of heat. It does work and every time. If under some situations it doesn't work, I can usually work out what it is that needs to be done, changing a fuse, replacing the plug or cable. But I get results when I turn the light on. But can it therefore be said that the Power of Prayer "works"? Not in the same context. Can it be said that mediumship "Works"? Not in the same context. Can it be said that ritual, charms and the like "Work"? No. Not in the same context. But the use of the phrase "It Works", due to its simplicity and stupidity, has helped (along with many other factors) lead the rest of the world into a state of calling all exploration into the supernatural, stupidity.

It is a peculiar form of insanity of the experimenters into the supernatural to take some small experience and then to extrapolate too far. Let us take the writings of mediums and spirit channelers. They have their experiences, they seem to feel of hear a message, a Ouija board maybe or automatic writing device acts to make something happen, they write them in books, which are sold in their millions to people from all walks of life. These works are snapped up a proof of life beyond the stars and life after death. But what actually happened here? The medium has had some experiences that they have jumped to the conclusion is 100% true and trustworthy (just like saying "It Works") and then they have forced their beliefs on the world as an article of faith. Now I am not saying that there is not life after death, as there is limited proof for or against that theory. I am not saying that there is not intelligent life somewhere out there in the cosmos, but I am saying that it is downright daft to believe that just because an experience happened that means that the experience is 100% proof of anything at all. That would be like me having had a bad experience in a relationship, deciding that all women were mad, dangerous bunny boilers and then choosing to live a life of celibacy forever. It is a narrow minded and unintelligent presupposition.

But, to choose to go out there into the unknown, to play about with these forces (be they real or not) and to see what happens, to see the whole thing as a long term character building exercise, that does me good on different levels and to increase the diversity of my life experience, maybe to give me some fun scary times and to give me moments that are beautiful beyond measure, that would actually make some sense, right? (And if you don't agree then carry on reading anyway, I might make you laugh if nothing else...)

So I hope that we can now proceed with our discussion of the supernatural without thinking that we have completely lost our minds, with a sense of reason behind what we do, and with the sure knowledge that we can see our experiences as just experiences and nothing more.

I have in the past defined the way that the world works into a few categories

X) a force or forces
Y) the method or mechanism by which they act and
Z) the result of these forces, the experience.

Now we can have experiences that can be classed as supernatural, but to jump to the conclusion that as a result of these experiences that we now have a great understanding of the X and Y factors involved is nonsense. Remember that I can pray and feel the presence of God when I do so, but I have to see that as just a experience and noting more than that, a Z factor. However, I cannot say that the experience is proof that a specific X force (God) has decided on that afternoon that Nick would be a great guy to have a chat with, a Y factor, thrust creating the experience of the presence of God when I pray, a Z factor. All I can say is that God seemed to appear to me when I prayed, not that God does or does not exist.

I can say that there is another variety of X factor, my artificially cultivated belief in God, another Y factor, getting on my knees in humility and prayer, that eventually created the sensation of God's presence, the Z factor. And when I got up from my knees after prayer, the belief in God left me an left me to be the normal and agnostic atheist that walks around the world not caring for matters of religion.

But if I find that at a certain time of day, I again do the same exercise, and get on my knees, pray, sense the presence of God, and THEN add some extra other factors into the mix such as a complex and deep visualization when in a state of religious joy, of maybe traveling in the Spirit body to go and see someone and then meet them, have a conversation with them, give them an object (say, a flower) and then return to my body to continue normal earthy life, and then to ask that person, the subject of my experiment, the next day what they dreamed of, and then to have them recount to you the detail of the dream that you "gave them" in great detail, even down to the colour flower that you gave them, then you have another peculiar Z factor that you can add to your understanding (or lack of it), of the way that the world works. I have done this in the past. Yes it is freaky, but I have done it all the same.

(Probably) The only tradition.

Within each and every school of occult thought there are three main aspects of learning, firstly that of meditative control, secondly that of the development of belief in a cosmology and theology (belief structure about how the world works and the various existences of the deities, spirits, demons etc) and thirdly that of educating the mind into a system of codes (symbology) that have meaning (the meanings are loosely labeled "energies"), such as shapes, colours, planets, plants, smells (incenses etc), signs and combinations of signs, personalities (as in the character of and personalties of the deities and spirits) and how to create (invoke, evoke) them.

This is probably the only similarity between each and every occult school of thought. There is no difference in my mind between a Christian counting rosary beads for hours on end and attempting to contact the very real God of his or her understanding, and a pagan magician sitting in the non constrictive cross legged posture and chanting the names of his or her deities to create and invoke their energies.

The only real problem is when you try and explain to either a Christian or a Pagan that they are doing the same thing as their "rivals" in another faith. If you do so you end up being criticized and even verbally or physically abused. The eternal debate for religious supremacy even occurs on the streets of your own suburb today. However, the actual acts remain the same. You may be thinking that what am talking about here is merely religious observance, rather than occultism, but I would have to say that there is the whole world of difference between preparing your mind and body to be able to create any supernatural effects as opposed to going to church for the social side of life.

Lets take another example, young boy in a Christian family is given plenty of days in Sunday school, is taken to a good C of E church school and only has Christian friends, every week and possibly every day he is exposed to the ideas of a certain interpretation of the Christian faith, the personality of Jesus, the miracles that he did and the observance of specific aspects of obedience and trust. Maybe every day his parents give him Christan videos about the life of Jesus and the parables and more mysteries of Jesus's life. With time the idea of the Christ personality, the energies (personality, imagery, ideas, concepts and the imaginary or spiritual "being", Jesus) become stronger and stronger in his mind. Often without him knowing it, he is performing an occult act, the veneration of energy force, a personality that is God made in his own mind. Just because the object of adoration is Jesus does not make the action of the veneration less of an occult activity than a Follower of Bacchus, Pan, the Angels, Santa Claus, Satan or Cthulu. Lets us say that in a state of crisis later in life, this Christin boy, now a man, gets on his knees and prays for salvation or to have some "evil" taken from him, if the stress be severe enough and the focus be intense enough, there is every chance that his God, the Lord Jesus, will actually appear to him in vision or in person, even manifest to physical appearance as solid as the computer monitor in front of me. But the Christian man will develop the understanding based on experience that he has seen the One True Christ and as such is blessed by God and that Jesus is real. However this reasoning is still delusional. There is no further evidence that Jesus is real in this situation than in any other. All we have is a phenomena, that's all and a subjective anecdotal one. If however the Christian man was to get on his knees again and pray for a result and for the vision of Christ for instance to appear to a friend of his or to sculpt the dreams of one of his family members as a result of the prayerful act after having received this Christ visitation, and this was done without the other person knowing it, And results were achieved, then and only then can we say that there are other factors at work here and that only under certain circumstances can this phenomena happen.

I am convinced that after having read this work and spent time practicing the development of spiritual ecstasy, you will be in a position to do the very same, not necessarily at will, but still successfully on occasion.

Now, be honest with yourself just for a minute, when you were walking past the bookshop or library and you decided to treat yourself to a few minutes out of the rain in the bookshop, what was it that drew you to this book? Was it a desire to "find out what the weird people are thinking these days?" or was it a slight suspicion that you wanted to try and achieve something "strange" for yourself to convince yourself of the reality of the supernatural? If you wanted the former, then you are at the wrong book as I don't actually believe in much, but if you wanted to work to create a supernatural effect, then you have a lot of work to go though. And unfortunately you have to cover all three parts of the tradition that I have mentioned above. Its more of a life long task rather than something that can be completed when the flatmates are at the pub.

The first and arguably the most problematic is the development of the knowledge of signs and energies as mentioned above. The reason that it is problematic is that many daft new agey books are written with many spells in them that "work". Now these spells are merely bastardisations of aspects of someone else's symbology (system of religious or spiritual symbols), not yours. So how the hell can you writing down the word abracadabra in a certain way, and lighting a candle really help you to get a new boyfriend? Basically it can't. The customer buys the book, loses a few dollars, applies a bit of faith to the exercise of writing the stuff down and doing the ritual, and then hey presto, sod all happens. And in exchange for a few dollars, the customer has wasted his or her time entirely, and probably made their family think that they should be committed.

The fact of the matter is, that what the customer in the bookshop will have done is to only apply a small part of the whole mystery of how to do any form of ritual or magickal work, essentially through the application of superstitious and not scientific methodology, and certainly not training the mind long term with meditation and prayer.

Alister Crowley wrote in one of his works that the Tree of Life (a system of categories arranged in a tree like diagram) should be seen as a filing cabinet, each drawer labeled in a certain way and as such, you have the freedom to apply all of your life experiences and thoughts and anything else that you can into your very own "filing cabinet" (however later in his writings he then suggested a very formulaic approach to the way that an individual should work thus going contrary the initial presupposition that you have freedom to create your own psychological world to use in your activities). Lets say a "sphere" (or category) has the "energy" of Earth associated with it. You can start by asking yourself, what is Earth? What colours are earth? What jobs are earthy? What have I done that is earthy? And then to expand the list ad infinitum and so begins a life work of creating a catalog of what it means to be "earthy". You also start to extrapolate, and say that what if water and earth mixed, how would that look? What would it feel like? And then to apply all the questions that you have asked yourself above to the idea of water and earth mixing. And so begins what is a life's worth of contemplation about all the other aspects of all the other "spheres" of the tree of life, elements, planetary energies and the like. But if you wished to create your own symbology, your own "tree" of life or other world model, then for crying out loud sake, do so! I certainly ain't gonna stop ya!

But, when you ask yourself about what personalities (deities, angels, spirits, demons) and animals are associated with the various "planetary" or elemental energies of a sphere, then you get into interesting territory, as then you are creating for yourself a cosmology, a world view, inhabited by "good" or "evil" (or any other combination of types of hierarchy of morality, personality or of anything else that you may wish) spirits, angels, demons and the like, you can go about naming them, creating bizarre "crossbreeds" of different creatures, lets say in your demon world of the sphere of earth, you create in your minds eye, a creature that is half bull and half man, one with the mentality of laborer that has gone "evil" and has to be constrained, you might choose a name similar to that of the Greek myth of the Minator, you might assign him symbols, some of which you have created and some of which you have seen elsewhere, you use a combination of the letters of His name as a mantra, and maybe you can even learn to control this imaginary force in your own imaginary world, until such time as you learn (through your own prayerful practice) how to "send" that force into someone else's mental or dream world...... and so you have learned to create a demon. Initially only in imagination, but with practice and perseverance, something that could actually have an effect, be it a subtle or possibly unpredictable or unreliable one, on the minds and lives of other humans.

But remember that the trap that any occultists gets into is to during the state of belief when you see and know that the spiritual force is there and you believe that it is real, is to carry that belief into the "real world". To do so would be to be insane. Many modern occultists deliberately cultivate laughter as a way of forgetting the concept from the conscious mind, or maybe placing it into perspective. It is a good idea to learn how to laugh and to do so after a ritual is totally complete. It is a methodology that seems to work quite well.

Just remember that if you want to get concrete results ever time, then ritual magick is not for you. There are too many factors and forces that seem to play a part, psychological factors, health factors and the like let alone the level of "development" that you yourself have. (Note: there is no known way of quantifying or qualifying what spiritual development is no matter what any grade "A" turkey says!) However the more that you play about with supernatural stuff, the more that you get used to knowing when the sensation, thought, emotion or experience that you have is the one that is going to help you to make something happen. This is all very experiential and no, you won' be able to master the whole universe that easy! Just see this as play, fun and if sometime really happens that scares the socks off you or gives you a feeling of ecstatic state or pleasure then it has all been worth it, but start off as seeing this as a hobby. The ramblings of the occultists speak in parables, often saying that the goal of magic is to become Godlike, but that is basically hooey, not based on fact and just based on occultists being blissed out of their minds on their own mis-understanding of the world, or even some nasty narcotic. (It should be noted that I once ended up drinking with a member of one of the alleged High Magic orders. Their emblem was a certain highland flower that was "revered for its occult properties". As it transpires, these alleged occult properties was that if the flower was dried and cured in certain way, when it was smoked, it would have a similar effect but milder, to cannabis. Maybe this explains more about the mentality of "high magic" occult orders then they might want the majority of the world to know....!)

Now, talking about meditative control. There are different states of mind and different ways of achieving them. It would be wise to develop a wide variety of techniques, through practicing them one at a time, designing a program of exercises for yourself that give you access to these states of mind, focusing one of them for 6 weeks, then moving onto another and so on, revisiting the ones that you used at an earlier time occasionally to keep your mind focused in developing the right states. There are the states of deep shamanic traveling, the states of calm and tranquil meditation and those associated with the higher brain wave frequencies that can also provide anomalous results.

Higher brainwave frequencies are not always better as it depends on the type of work that you want to do and the state of mind that you need to be able to generate. If you are an epileptic or have any other seizure complaint, then don't bother with even trying states of an ecstatic nature as it can bring about the fits.

No matter which exercises you are trying the main thing is to practice an practice on a regular basis, ideally at the same time of day and the same times of the week so as to firstly treat your brain as a muscle that needs to be trained in a certain way for the purpose of being able to carry out specific tasks and secondly to incorporate the exercise into your circadian rhythms so that it becomes easier to enter into those states of mind when you need to.

Remember that when you are learning any mental task, be it a new language, a new game, even learning to walk, you are teaching the brain to work in a new way, forcing the neurons to grow in certain patterns that will help to facilitate the tasks at hand. The more that you do specific mental exercises, the more heavily ingrained they become into your brain, they become a part of you, like a limb, or a new organ.

For instance, I am used to prayer as an exercise, I do it daily, I am used to cultivating the belief in God and used to sensing the seemingly very real presence of God when I pray. If I was to see this in a purely psychological and neurological point of view, I have trained my brain to operate in a certain way so that it has became easier and easier to create the phenomena to my apparent senses, of the presence of God, but it is still no evidence of the existence of God either way. If I stop praying for a period of a few months, for instance, I seem to loose the skill and as such I have to regain it with more "practice". It is my firm understanding that there is no such thing as a "powerful magician" or "powerful psychic" but just people who have specialized in certain psychological exercises, for instance a person who has spent their entire life learning divination will be better at it than a person who has dedicated their entire life to learning spiritual healing. Just as a person who has dedicated their entire life to understanding how to play chess will be better it it than a person who has dedicated their entire life to learning how to play Texas Hold 'em Poker. Also temperament and makeup play an important role too. I do not feel that one can simplify this factor down into basic elements or human personality typology, it is down to your own trial and error. You can work at observing your own behavior and learning from that which occult skills you feel you can develop with greater ease, be is psychometry, healing, telepathy and the like. It is possible that with extra work one can learn a greater repertoire of psychological skills thus becoming a greater psychic all rounder, but again that will require work.

But what are the states of mind and how do you know that you are in them when you practice them? This is where the normal scientific community has provided us with tools that can help us to explore the world of our own minds with greater ease. The technology is called Brain Wave Entrainment, and it uses a combination of light and sounds (in a similar way as shamanic drumming) to adjust the workings of the human brain with great accuracy. It is probable (but by no means certain) that brain wave activity is the only really measurable phenomena that occultists can use to assess their progress. For instance, knowing that people who perform shamanic healing and divination work are typically in a state of consciousness that can be typified by a predominance of the 4.5 cycles per second frequency in their brain and to experience sound and or light that seems to operate at that frequency during their various ceremonials, surely it would be beneficial for you to use strobe light and pulsing tones at that frequency to help you to enter into that same state of mind? If states of spiritual ecstasy and the precursor states of astral projection occur in the Gamma frequency band of over 30 cycles per second, surely if you wished to experiment with that technique, you should get used to that brainwave frequency? If you wished to reach a state of consciousness that was the same as the most skilled meditators and was the state of total calm and tranquility characterized by the 7.83 cycles per second frequency, surely it would be necessary to develop that state of mind too?

You can get brain wave entrainment technology in the form of binaural beat generators, mind machine strobe light devices and many more. You can buy some CDs that provide the same states of consciousness as defined above, some that use the "audiostrobe" signals that communicate to a mind machine and make the strobes flash at the same frequency as the sounds too if you so desire. But the fact is that as you explore the frequencies more and more, you realize that there is a certain "mood", "texture" or emotion associated with the different frequencies and as you come to recognize what these "moods" are, you can using concentration and memory re-evoke them when you need them, but again that takes practice, practice and more bloomin' practice!

But, you don't just use the strobe lights and all that jazz, you learn to practice with mantras, drumming, cymbals, prayer wheels, rosaries and kinds of manners of inexpensive quaint religious toys from the junk stores and new agey shops that you visit. Remember that every tool that people of religion use has a mind altering aspect to them, all the prayers, meditations and mantras that they use are about creating in the mind of the Believer the state of being in direct communication or communion with the Divine forces of the belief systems of the nations, races, religions who own those religious tools.

You get yourself a diary or a file, and make notes on a regular basis of ALL the factors that went into the experience, and you make notes in a rigorous and honest way as to what you did (no-one else is going to see your ramblings so be

100% honest!), the way that you were thinking, the way that you were feeling and all the rest. Maybe even noting your diet and nutritional intake throughout the year as to highlight any allergy or nutritional factors that might contribute to the effect on the days when you do your experiment, you make notes of the time that you went to bed, the time that you got up and how well you slept (in great detail) as that can also affect the result, you include any details of medications that you were taking at the time. After all, just like birdwatchers observe the increases and decreases in various species over time, you will be watching another important aspect of the natural world, namely you and your experiences. Maybe after each week, month, or quarter year, you review your notes and start to get a feeling for what is happening, you start to connect ideas and think about how certain phenomena occur, you experiment further and see if you can recreate the same experience again, and if you can't, then you look closely at what was happening bodily, psychologically and emotionally, what moods you were in, what state of mind you had and how you created it.

You take great pains to only turn your belief on during the time that you are experimenting. And when the experiment is over, you try and deliberately disbelief what you had experienced. You laugh with it, at it and take the mickey out of yourself for even trying, that is the way that you stop yourself from developing beliefs or other disorders that could be damaging to yourself later on in life.

Remember that what you are not doing is being religious, although you may be creating a combination of ideas, thoughts and feelings (many of a religious or quasi religious nature) that you build up over time, there is no way of concretely proving that there is a real truth here, that you are uncovering a fact about the way that the physical and spiritual world is working at all. All you are doing in reality is having fun, playing about and enjoying it to the full (at this stage anyway!). There is no point in stating that just because I do a certain exercise that it proves that anything in the supernatural world exists at all. But we can observe and look out for strange coincidences that occur, and use them for moments of pondering and wonderment.

Now, as I have suggested, no-one can guarantee any specific 100% accurate and targeted results, but there are people who claim to have that level of accuracy in their skills. If these people are sincere in their beliefs, then one can only assume that they lack the ability to rationally and objectively look at what they are doing and how they are working, or their primary purpose is to do damage to others. Although it must be great for everyone to be living in a world of greater religious tolerance, this does have its downsides. The primary one is that of the opening of vulnerability, and that doesn't mean that the people in question have to be needy or vulnerable by nature, but just plain human. I have known people with PHD and Masters qualifications who were great business owners and doing rather well for themselves, who still found that they would have their minds adjusted by people who made claims to powers or religious authority. This abuse seems to occur in many different levels, firstly that of the social group of spiritual or religious people, whereby one or more than one individual will seek to find a character that seems to be suitable for exploitation, be they a rich and intelligent person or a poor and sickly one, and then make claims to skill and power, or the authority of Jesus (or any other being from any belief system) etc., and will then experiment with the individual until the individual ceases or have the power of rational thought and then becomes a tool or puppet for the religious or spiritual nut. Now this can be done either because of the belief system of the group, where it is acceptable behavior to adjust the minds of others, or it can be much more unsavory. Just as a fledgling killer might experiment on some lesser species prior to exploring the realm of human killing, the fledgling cult leader and brainwasher experiments on what he considers to be lesser humans until such time as he feels he has gained the ability to control larger groups of humans for his benefit. Each success making his psychological sickness deeper and stronger and each failure creating resentment that also feeds on the desire to succeed more and more. These people are probably incurable and all pains must be taken to keep them the hell away from you or for you to keep the hell away from them. Although I don't like to use the monochrome ideas about good versus evil, I have to say that the ones who use their minds and lives in this way simply can't be good.

One of the symptoms of this type of sickness is the claim to be able to "just do" nearly any form of supernatural activity, without self training, practice or sufficient humility to be able to say "I can't guarantee results". It is much wiser for person to say that this is an experiment and we are doing it for fun and enjoyment. Some people say that it is good for occultists to work together. I seriously caution against this as that can make you really rather unhappy as you get assaulted for having independent thought, being able to think for yourself and having the desire to find out, experiment and enjoy your occultism. Be careful as there are many fledgling cult leaders out there in the world. Especially in various new agey religions that make claim to spell casting, magick and the like.

Visualization.

Now the subject of visualization has been touched upon by many occultists thought the world. By visualization, I mean something a little more than just a daydream, something more than an imaginary excursion to a fantasy holiday home, but more of a deep and almost real hallucinatory experience, but somehow strangely even more then that, something that you don't just visualize, but can "feel" too. To "sense", "feel" and "see" simultaneously. It is true for instance, that the temporary hallucinations that we all experience when asleep (and therefore in an altered state of consciousness), dreams, can be vivid and powerful, but how comfortable do you feel with the idea of having them when you are awake and lucid? How used to you are at having visual experiences that you can almost feel and sense as being real?

Whenever I have used visualization in my occult work it has been always in a state of mind that is more then just my normal one. It seems to work best when I have trained myself on a mind machine in the theta frequencies around the 4.5 cycles per second frequency, an sometimes at the higher ones of 7.83 (Schumann resonance, the frequency that the Earths own electromagnetic field resonates at, roughly speaking) and, for astral projection type experiences, at the gamma frequencies above 30 Hz. No matter what the exercise, the state of visualization has to be rather intense, believable and almost "real". The more that you experiment with visualization and practice holding the concentration on the visual imagery, you are most definitely learning how to hold the mind at certain brainwave frequencies (relative to the "mood" of the experiment) almost to the exclusion of all others. For instance if you are skilled at visualization and you wished to try and astral projection experience, you would lie on the bed with your arms at the sides, breath as naturally as your body wishes, but using your meditative skill to slow the body down as well as steadily generating for yourself the ecstatic state of buoyancy, floating, it seems euphoric, and it is the higher brain wave activity frequencies of the gamma range. You combine the cultivation of the euphoric flying dream state of mind with the visualization of the phantom which is identical to your own body, lifting itself out of the physical shell and moving slowly and steadily upwards. You avoid using words to describe the things that you are visualizing and try and keep everything down to non verbal visualization. You hold your concentration on the activity of moving upwards ever upwards as well as holding the "mood" as ecstatic and serene, and with further practice you may well develop the full astral externalization of the phantom. But, lets say just for arguments sake you don't manage to get the full symptoms as described in Muldoon and Carrington's "The Projection of the Astral Body", but you still want to go for a "wander" about. You keep the visualization strong, you are visualizing everything that would be in your own field of view if you were standing or floating where the astral phantom (imaginary body) is. You choose to walk about the house or block of flats where you live, taking mental notes of the things that you see as you go along. Maybe you notice that a certain cup that should be in the drainer happens to be in the living room. Then after the experience, it transpires that the cup in question had been used by one of your flatmate's and not put back! What you would have done without knowing it was a feat of divination using remote viewing. But, you can't put pressure on yourself to make a statement that "every time I do this thing such and such happens" as that would be untrue, you can only state that you did certain exercise, experienced certain phenomena, and then reported the results. Believers in the psychological creed would say that you already knew that the flatmate was likely to use that cup anyway and you were only "seeing" what your deep subconscious mind already knew. But the more that you play about with the exercise, the more that you realize that there is more to this experience than meets the eye. My point in this example is that the vivid visualization under these conditions was created by the skilled use of high "resolution" visualization under deep meditative or hypnotic conditions. Such a feat of concentration, all non verbal, would require a lot of brain wave activity and as such you would need to have practiced for a long time, be well nourished and have great powers of concentration.

But once you have developed a suitable toy box jam packed full of things to play with, religious artifacts, crystals of all sorts, crystal balls, objects of meditation, Ouija boards and pendulums, tarot packs and rune stones, the next thing to think about is what on earth to do with them. And more importantly, what it is you want to achieve. By now you should have experienced and experimented with different states of consciousness, different states of mind and will probably have had a whale of a time doing so. But what was the goal, what was the original reason for experimenting with the occult? What did you wish to achieve? With any luck you probably don't know (because if you already had a fixed goal such as winning the lottery or getting over a disease that you were born with, you probably will be completely dissatisfied and disgruntled by now) and a such you are in the right state to continue playing about, having fun with supernatural ideas.

The skill sets of an occultist can be broken down into a number of different subsections or headings. Many of which overlap a leedle.

Let us return for the moment to astral projection and remote viewing. There seems to be a similarity between the various stories that have occurred over time. Firstly astral projection is defined as making ones own ghost leave the body for a period of time and then to return to the physical so that the human can recount the story or make notes and the like. According to the English translation of the book that the Inquisition used to define witchcraft, the Malleus, the witches would use system of visualization, visualizing the soul energy as a blue ectoplasm that would extend out of the nostrils and then form into the spirit outside of the body. In the Muldoon and Carrington text on the subject, the ectoplasm leaves the body via a cable that extends from the forehead of the physical person (being near a major nervous center, the brain) and then connects to the astral body, the phantom, at the back of the head.

You might as well say that, for the purposes of convenience and to preserve your own sanity, that both of these views are, to a certain degree, untrue, but can still be useful belief structures that you can accept, use and then discard, that are used to help you to be able to achieve the same phenomena. Remember that you are doing this for a laugh and not for any real 100% solid evidence, it is just for fun. But you are going to use your diary or file to write down all the things that you have experienced during the experiment and leave nothing out, just in case you do experience something really curious......... :)

The things that you should be asking yourself here are which models of supernatural reality are you going to use? Which belief structures? Are you going to base them on other people's or use your own? How are you gong to relax prior to doing the actual work? What are you going to do to stop yourself from being afraid of any spiritual intrusions (this is covered later in this essay)? How are you going to measure any success or failure? How are you gong to define anomalous experiences that you could learn from? What time of day are you going to do the experiment in? How often are you going to experiment and how will you fit that into your daily routine without creating any suspicion?

Then, after many months of practice with the exercises mentioned above and in the section on visualization, lets say that you become aware that it would be fun and pleasurable to visit an exhibition in a certain major town in your astral body. An exhibition that you have never visited before, but plan on visiting after the astral projection or remote viewing exercise is over, just to see whether there is any connection between your astral excursions and the physical reality of what was there at, or around, that time.

You do some research, you look into the names of the streets that the exhibition hall is in, you learn the way that you could get there if you were traveling on foot, you learn how far away it is and possibly even researching what the outside of the exhibition hall building looks like from photographs on the Internet. You create in your minds eye a journey of the whole situation, how you would get there, how fast and what route the astral body would take. You become obsessed with the success of the exercise, and the ways in which the astral would go to get to the exhibition hall. Being obsessive is important with astral projection exercises like this, I can't even begin to explain why.

You move on to the exercise proper, with the stage of relaxation, for this astral projection to work you will need the physical to be as close to being totally relaxed as is possible as during the exercise you will be focusing your mental powers on the activity of moving the astral and not the physical. You have a nice hot bath before hand, making the body relaxed and supple, you get into clothing that is non constrictive and comfortable, then either lying or sitting in a position in which you can get totally relaxed, you close your eyes.

Move on to a visualization exercise that allows you to generate a form of mind and body awareness, a awareness of your astral and physical shape. Visualize a ball of brilliant white light above your head, it is spherical and only just slightly smaller than your own head, visualize it traveling down through the head and illuminating the entire head with light, then move onward to visualizing the ball of light hovering between the shoulder blades at the foot of the neck, it then moves down the right arm to the fingers and back to between the shoulder blades, having illuminated the entire arm with brilliant white light, do the same with the left arm, and then the chest and abdomen, then the right leg and then the left leg. The ball of light then comes to rest at the pelvis prior to moving pack up the body to above the top of the head prior to vanishing. This exercise doesn't just give you mind and body awareness, but gives you the ability to start the brain moving in meditative and visualization states of consciousness, vital for success!

As the early stages of an astral projection is often characterized by the higher frequency brain wave activities, the gamma state, you focus the mind on the emotion of ecstatic euphoria, but calm and serene. The state of mind of a flying dream. Then start to visualize a replica of your own physical self emerging from within the physical. Slowly at first, but with perseverance the astral will become free. You may experience sensations such as the astral "snapping back" into place, or maybe vibratory sensation, the heartbeat in the back of the head and a number of other sensations. Make mental notes of them and persist with the visualization, allow the astral to move parallel to the resting physical further and further out of the body until the imaginary body, the astral, is maybe 4 – 5 feet above the physical. Continue with the visualization, make it slide out sideways to a distance of about 5 – 10 feet from the bed where your physical is lying and then to slowly move towards an upright position and to descend gracefully to the floor level. Be sure as to not get to close to the physical frame again as that can bring the imaginary astral body back in to the physical. Incidentally the sensation of walking a bit erratically and almost as if drunk when near the physical is a symptom of a "real" projection for reasons that Muldoon and Carrington explained, but we need not extrapolate to the same conclusions as Mr Muldoon did about the astral cable.

At this point in your visualization, you start your journey. By now you should know the route and how the astral is supposed to go there, in your minds eye, travel there, you know which routes to go down, which hills to fly over and how to get there. Make sure that you take mental notes as to anything odd or different, any details that pop into your minds eye whilst going on this imaginary trip. When you "arrive there" go up the entrance steps, walk in the door, be open and have a look around, take mental notes as to the floor plan, any shapes and symbols that come to your minds eye, the exhibits and the postures of the mannequins, the colours of logos and corporate insignias. Take as long as you like to do this exercise, just in imagination and visualization only, and then when you are done, just fly back home the same way that you flew out to the exhibition hall. Remember to bring your astral body back into the physical through visualizing its return into the physical frame. You may notice sensation of warmth as the astral coincides with the physical. When you are done, get up, massage the hands and stretch the legs or whatever you wish to do to make yourself feel like you are back and alive again in the physical space. Then get straight to your diary or file and make notes of every step of the journey and what happened in the "trip". Then, go and visit the exhibition hall for "real" in the physical body, taking your notes with you and trying to see where the similarities and differences were between the two events. Maybe research what was there the previous month and the coming month and see if there was a time perception aspect here too. You may well be pleasantly surprised at the result. But it takes practice to be able to do this relatively reliably. And each time you try it, there will be some "hits" and some "misses" but that is also all part of the fun! With time you will be getting a more in depth understanding of how to do the exercise better and better. Try visiting different places and visiting different people at times of the day when you know that they will be asleep, try talking to their sleeping bodies through this method and then ask them what they dreamed off that night..... It can be really rather entertaining the results that you may get.

However I would caution you not to do this when you are feeling lustful and in need of some kind of sexual gratification. It can create rather disconcerting results indeed.

Another variation on a theme here is the transformation of a portion of astral energy into an animal that then goes out of the body's astral energy and does the bidding of the magician. Whether this is made up of a portion of your own astral energy or not or whether this is your own astral body that has become an animal is purely theoretical and one cannot say either way. Whether indeed this creation merely exists telepathically (in the "ether"), again we can only hazard a guess, but no matter what, the ideas remain the same, but you have the power to turn this creation into a separate entity in its own right or to have this as a form that your own sense of perception travels in, like your own astral body turned into an animal.

Lets say that for your own personal reasons you have an interest in traveling into the astral in the form of a black cat. As well as all the other complexities of visualization that I have mentioned above, you would have to take a detailed and in depth analysis of cats, the shape and form of cats, the sheen of the fur, the facial expression, the musculature and the skeleton and to compare and contrast that with the skeleton of a human. You will have to develop a certain level of unnatural obsession with cats. To cover the walls of your bedroom with images of cats, to watch videos and films about cats and their behavior and their language, the way that they move. Become an obsessive expert on the cat! (this could take months). Then use your skills with visualization to allow yourself to change the shape of the spiritual from that you take up, to make the ears pointy and to move them to the tops of the head, to stretch the palms of the hands to make the lower limbs of the cat and to extend forward the rib cage, develop a deep understanding from science, from fiction and from your own deep and dark imagination as to how your own form would change to that of a cat, imagine yourself being the cat an walking like a cat. (I am only using the idea of a cat here by example, there is no reason why you should not use any other creature be it real, as in the cat example, or imagined, such as a werewolf or dragon.....)

Once your obsession with feline forms has been sufficiently fortified, you have a choice, you can either use the cat as a means by which you travel astrally around the neighborhood, or you can create the cat spirit as a separate entity to yourself. If we were to temporarily hijack the belief that the body is full of a kind of fluid plasma energy and that the energy can be sent out of certain organs of nervous system activity such as in this case, the solar plexus just below where the ribs divide. Lets say that for a period of 40 nights, you take one hour a day and in each one hour, you use the visualization skill that you have gained to create the cat spirit, visualizing a stream of blue light emerging from the solar plexus, and then centering into the same space of the room on each and every single night. You imagine that the cat shape is growing, like a Siamese twin of yours, taking shape and from, becoming the cat, and linked to the body purely by the beam of blue light emanating from the solar plexus. You give it a name and make the spirit stronger in your meditations even to the point occasionally when you can hear it mewing, you talk to it in your mind, give it purpose, attributes a character and personality, feed it with a saucer of milk stroke it and make it feel loved and wanted, but all the time telling the cat that it is separate from you an that it gains pleasure from following your orders. You continue to do this time and time again until the 40 nights are up and the cat is fully "born". (some occultists would also fortify the spiritual creature by giving it biological energies from blood, saliva and other bodily fluids, but I feel that this might be a little unnecessary!). Periodically, give the form extra "food" through calling it and again talking to it as if it were a real live physical cat, but then in other meditations, start giving it orders and sending it out to do your work, something that a cat might be good at, like giving comfort to an elderly relative, or getting rid of some unwanted force that is giving you nightmares through stalking it and hunting it down, or indeed to give an enemy of yours nightmares just for the hell of it.... Its your cat, do what you want with it! These spiritual forces seem to take time to create and a lot of work to keep "alive", but when they are fully formed, you may find that you get cat like weights on the bed at night and even feeling the cat rubbing its body against your legs whist you sit up at night and watch TV. You will find yourself being haunted by your own creation, but that isn't quite as harrowing as it sounds! Remember that every time you feed, strengthen, fortify, call or send your cat, spirit or whatever, go back to your non believing state afterwards and then rationally and objectively write down every step of the experience in the notes. Remember to do this honestly and thoroughly otherwise you won't be able to get a real and precise understanding as to what the heck you are doing. Note down the state of mind that you were in, the brain wave frequency pattern (AKA state of mind) that you believed yourself to be in at that time and all the rest. Whatever results you get, write them down. Even the most trivial thing can become really important later on as you get more of an experiential understanding as to what you are playing with.

Banishing and spiritual protection.

Banishing rituals have been greatly misunderstood over time. Phil Hine, the Chaos magick author said once that the activity of banishing is not to tell negative energies to go away, but it is a centering exercise in much the same way as the visualization of white light was in the astral projection exercise mentioned previously. So we have to see the exercise in perspective. Believers in the aura state that banishing ritual is essentially there to protect the aura from attack, to fortify the aura and to make yourself stronger. It might have this effect, but either way it seems to give one a sense of calm and focus. To take any distractions and distracting thoughts and to put them aside for the purposes of the magical work that you are about to do. So, therefore, banishing rituals are completely separate from the school of thought that rules over exorcisms. One could even say that the term banishing is and has been misused.
There seems to be two different types of banishing, one that is focused on the

idea of centering the mind and aura of the practitioner alone, and the other that is centered on preparing a place so that the whole place, is a calm and relaxed place to perform magical activities. In the former case, each technique no mater what seems to have as its goal to increase the mind/body awareness as in the visualization of white light as mentioned in the above astral projection visualization, and to have the "white protective light" surrounding the practitioner to approximately arms length. The latter method seems to be about placing energy plasma beings, forms or shapes at the cardinal points and then asking them to stay there until the time that the ceremony is over. Whichever methods that you use will depend to what degree that you can convince yourself that the actual activity is working at all, and to what degree you need to rely upon gestures rather than visualization.

It doesn't really matter two figs which method you use, so long as when you turn on the state of believing in what you do, you believe 100% in the exercise that you are doing. As most people tend to experiment alone, and possibly at a time when others in the household are asleep, maybe a method that is done in total silence would be best for me to recommend to you. Remember that this exercise not only creates the sense of being "centered" but also enhances mind and body awareness and awareness of the space that you are working in, as well as stimulation the ability to concentrate at an altered state of consciousness and visualize that is essential to any occult activity of this type. Remember also that many people do this before and after any occult exercise so as to state to your own subconscious mind the beginnings of the "supernatural space" and the return to normal waking consciousness. So it is something that you might want to practice before you do astral projection work, the creation of spirits and the like.

Stand and face any particular compass point that you feel is holy. If you don't know which direction is holy anyway and want to add a bit of a spooky flair to the whole event, light a candle and place it on the table. Start facing that candle with your arms by your side and with the heels together like one standing to attention. Take an in breath and extend the index finger of your dominant hand upwards to above your head, now as you exhale draw and visualize simultaneously a beam of white light descending from above your head, down through your head and then extending to the floor. Visualize the beam of light brightly, take time over it and make sure that the beam is bright and powerful. Then clasp the hands at your chest and extend a beam of light outward from your chest to arms length, again drawing and exhaling as you do so. Clasp your hands at you chest again, turn 90 degrees to the right and repeat the exercise of extending a beam of light outwards exhaling as you do so, turn another 90 degrees, repeat and one more time so that the final visualization is that of singular beam of light descending from above through you body and 4 "arms" of light extending outward to the 4 quarters. Then take another massive in breath and then as you exhale (slowly) visualize a ball of light expanding from the point where the arms of light join and expending to take up your whole aura at arms length. Finally keep the visualization for a moment and place the hands in prayer position at the center of the chest. You should now feel calm and balanced centered and closer to at one with your body and mind. You can do this (when alone and in doors!) every time you feel a bit upset and uptight about anything or you are experiencing fear from the possibility of psychic attack. Some people do this whenever they wake up to declare the start of the day and again at bedtime to declare the end of the day. The more that you do it, the better that you get at the exercise, visualization and body and mind awareness, so its good for that as well as making you feel good. I call this one the "Jack of Light" as the visualization seems like a jack as in a game of jacks with the bouncy ball.

The other method is a little more curious, it is the casting of the circle, probably the only singular ritual exercise that seems to be in all occult traditions simultaneously. There are similarities of theory and practice in each and every cultural strain that is present on the face of the planet. No matter which country the magical practice comes from, and despite ceremonial differences, the theory and methods have striking similarities. In each case, the ritualist prays for and/or conjours a spiritual force, elemental, personality, spirit or demon to be present at the various cardinal points of the compass, in each case they are welcomed and invoked with a sign or symbol that seems to represent to the mind of the people doing the ritual, a welcoming of their energy and a method of communicating that they (the spiritual forces) are present to the minds of the followers. At the end of the ceremony, the spiritual force is banished by another symbol that is used to communicate to the spiritual force that the ritual is over and that is it time to go home. The circle itself has been likened to the ring of Solomon in the greater and lesser keys of Solomon and it is attributed the power by the believers of various occult strains of thought the ability to keep unwanted spirits out. Whether it actually does this or not is for you to choose to believe during and disbelieve after!

Do take into account that the actual theology of every culture has its variances, and so does yours! So take into account that the method of circle casting that I am outlining here is just one singular method. You are more than free to use any different symbols that you see fit and fit in with the world view that you have been developing as you have been practicing and developing your own occult world view as mentioned in the earlier pages of this book. I did however hear an interesting anecdote once that an EMF meter, a measuring device for spotting and the Electromagnetic field that is emanated from household appliances, wiring and even organic material, was placed in the center of the circle prior to its casting. When the circle was sealed, the EMF meter registered a much lower level of electromagnetic energy. The needle sprang back to its previous position when the circle was closed down, after the ceremony. Maybe this suggests that the circle has more power than just on the minds and auras of the participants in the ritual? Maybe the circle DOES keep out unwanted influences? However this was just an anecdote. You are free to draw your own conclusions.

For this particular ritual, I have decided to use circles, drawn clockwise to symbolize invocation and anticlockwise to symbolize exorcism (sending the forces back home). Do take into account that this is just one idea that I am presenting here, occultists use a wide variety of symbols, for instance pentagrams drawn in certain ways having different meanings than when drawn in another way and so on, but that is merely the system that they use, the mechanism mentioned below is the same, but the symbology is different. So long as it suits the system of magick that you have devised and the symbols make sense to you then that is fine and essentially all that will be required of you. Remember, this is to be fun at any rate so don't worry about whether this is right or wrong, there is NO such thing as an actual technique. Also the spiritual energies and personalities, the names of the spirits are going to be different no matter what culture they come from, the names that are presented here are just names, see them as blank spaces that you can fill with the energies and names of the spiritual forces that you create. Likewise the tools that are mentioned here, the ritual artifacts, you don't have to use the same ones that I am mentioning. I am supposed to be helping you to learn how to play with occultism and, as such you must remain in control of what you are choosing to believe and disbelieve at any time when you are doing your own rituals. Also remember that this is also to be considered as a training exercise, it allows you to feel the presence and power of the spiritual energy, to know what it feels like to do an invocation and to make an effect that is gong to work to your benefit though getting experiential knowledge of magick.

Practitioners of Wicca will probably find this model most familiar ;)
I call this one the "Circle of Rings".

In this ritual I am making the assumption that you have a table that you can burn a candle on and smaller occasional tables at the other 3 cardinal compass points. You start with one candle already lit (for convenience we will call this the Altar candle) on the main Eastern most table, with another unlit beside it, and one other candle on the other occasional tables in the other cardinal points.

You can start either by dong the ball of light visualization or maybe the Jack of

Light ritual itself just to center and focus yourself. Then walk around the area once clockwise. Say "By the powers invested in me I am here to perform this ritual to invoke the Guardian spiritual forces of the Four Corners. In the name of He who has given me this power I invoke the Four Corners by Light and Fire."

Stand facing the direction of the alter candle, east, and then draw a large circle at about arms length starting at the top and going around clockwise. As you do so recite "By the powers I posses and In the name of He who has given me this power I invoke and Conjour Thee, Angel of the East" Light the eastern most candle with the flame from the Altar candle. Then carry the altar candle round to the next position clockwise, recite " By the powers I posses and In the name of He who has given me this power I invoke and Conjour Thee, Angel of the South" again as you draw a circle as before. Light the southern candle. Then carry the altar candle round to the next position clockwise, recite " By the powers I posses and In the name of He who has given me this power I invoke and Conjor Thee, Angel of the West" again as you draw a circle as before. Light the western candle. Then carry the altar candle round to the next position clockwise, recite " By the powers I posses and In the name of He who has given me this power I invoke and Conjor Thee, Angel of the North" again as you draw a circle as before. Light the Northern candle. Return to the Eastern most position placing the alter candle back on the alter area on the eastern table. Now stand in the middle of the area that you are "working" in, inhale deeply and then extend the index finger of the dominant hand outwards and draw a circle of light from east, round the other circles and back to east again and as you do so, exhale and visualize the circle of light joining all the others. Facing east recite "The One who hast give me this power be above me, the Angel of the South be to my right the angel of the North be to my left, Behind me the the Angel of the West and before me be the Angel of the East. I am now in the place where Spirits dance and the Demons are subdued. Amen!" If with each invocation of the Angels you actually visualize the presence of an angelic being standing there and guarding the circle, then that will add an extra bit of something to the whole experience.

If you have never done one of these ceremonies before, what you need to do is to turn your mind to the feelings that arise when you are dong this. Do you get a feeling of presence? Do you get a "church like" feeling when the circle is sealed by light? Did you get a strange sensation when you exhaled and sealed the circle? What could that be due to? Which models of the universe that you have read about could explain that sensation?

Theory has it that you have now prepared the area to be used for magical or occult work of any type or sort. You have created a space that feels safe and has the added advantage of being illuminated by candles, thus making the whole atmosphere seem more spiritual, possibly spookier and somehow nicer for strange things to happen in. Typically, after "casting" one of these circles you would now start by invoking deities, raising energy and preparing to send the energy to a certain place or person for the purposes of giving you the results that you have been seeking, maybe performing sympathetic magick using items that represent people or something of substance happening to a person, like the reunification of lovers. This circle casting can be a good way of ritually preparing an area prior to creating the cat spirit, somewhere that the spiritual force will feel at home, comfortable and non threatened by outside forces. It can be a place to do some remote viewing or astral projection from and a place to have a séance for the purposes of speaking to the dead or any supernatural beings that you choose to believe in at that time.

However, after each action that you do, you close the circle down afterwards, which is basically the reverse of what you did before, you do everything backwards apart from speaking backwards. You exorcise the spirits through drawing counter clockwise circles, you do them in reverse order, instead of lighting the candles in order, you extinguish them in reverse order. Instead off exhaling and drawing the line of light around the circle, you inhale and "suck" the light back up your arm and into your body. Instead of conjuring the spiritual forces, you banish them back to whence they came, kindly and politely but sternly, but you still do it. Instead of visualizing the light appearing you visualize it disappearing etc etc. then maybe follow that with the Jack of Light that I mentioned earlier. Then once the experience is over, you go straight back to the diary or notes and wrote down all th small details of what happened, so you have a record of your progress and what you are coming to believe and disbelieve. Then you choose to enter into a state of disbelief and don't worry about anything occult for the rest of the day at all. Remember that this is just an experience and noting more, and as such you start to learn how to take careful notes on what you are doing, but you are equally careful not to jumped to any conclusions as to the reality of any supernatural experience. However, despite the fact that I say this, there is always a certain degree of fun to be had when one does some form of occult activity, gets unexpected "results" and then ends up getting scared witless.

Lets say for arguments sake that the magician (you maybe) has many many hours to spare and is bored as hell. Knowing that you won't be disturbed you decide to try to summon a spiritual force. You decide that you will do a similar circle casting as mentioned above, but you add another variation, you create a section of the room inside the circle, a triangle of candles that the spiritual force will get trapped in and can't harm you. You use a paper knife as a ritual dagger to draw the invocation circles and then, you use a symbol of the spiritual force that you wish to summon, you take his name and remove any repeating letters and then jumble them up to provide a nonsense word that is to be the mantra to be used to bring forth the energy of that spirit. You sit and chant the mantra in the silence of the house after sunset for more than 30 minutes increasing the speed and ferocity that you chant, increasing the loudness of the chanting, getting pleasure from doing so, and then at the climax (at 30 minutes), you take out the ritual dagger and then draw a symbol that you associate with his name and "energy" over the triangle and summon him forth. The atmosphere in the room somehow changes and a feeling that there is some kind of presence in the room grows stronger and stronger. You point the dagger at the "spirit" and give it an order, and then tell it to go back from whence it came, fulfilling your desire as it does so, whilst drawing his invocation sign backwards. You do your closing of the circle, make a few notes about the sensation of the presence and then laugh it off as good fun and entertainment.

You go to bed that night and as you are slowly drifting off to sleep, you feel a weight on your shoulder and thigh, you open your eyes and see a dark shadowy figure leaning over your bed, he has one hand on your thigh and one on your shoulder. You scream and he vanishes as if he was never there, but the strange feeling of a presence in the room remains. From then on you have fitful dreams and that figure comes to you again and then gives you messages, that you write down, some of which are powerful and give you direction, and some are more disturbing and that you choose not to believe in, but the spirit stays with you for a long time to come. This is what happened to me in the early days. Also the thing that I commanded the spirit to do, actually did occur. However I feel that it would be rash for me to jump to conclusions and state that the spirit did the work for me. What I would state is that the experience was one that I most certainly would not trade for anything on Gods Earth. It was enlightening, entertaining and frightening all at the same time. The experience will always be there to make me wonder about the greater existence outside of th physical and whether God really has provided us humans with Angels, Spirits, and Demons to help Humankind along in its development. I know it is such a shame that I am a rational thinker and as such I cannot extrapolate from the experience further than the fact that it was just an experience. :(

Focusing and Moving the spiritual energy, The Methods and Theories behind the Eucharist and Talismanic activity

During the Christian Mass, the communion, the priest often draws the sign of the cross over the wine and the bread prior to giving that to the congregation. Is that just symbolic or is there something more to it than that? Is there a way that you can test and play about with the idea of blessing and otherwise affecting the properties of an object via psychic means?

Lets start by breaking down the activity into its constituent parts. The priest has spent many years in the church, he has gone through ordination and has discussed the concepts of the life of Christ Jesus, the deity that he worships, the energy of that supernatural being. The priest has gained a good understanding of what the personality, colours and ideas associated with Jesus are. And then we find him, one who is often in a state of prayer, an altered state of consciousness where he tries and makes himself full of worthiness to be able to receive the Holy Spirit, an then he goes about drawing the symbol that he associates with the energy and personality of the Christ being over the Wine and Bread of the mass. Occultists would say that he has actively changed the properties of the wine and bread in away that is kind of subtle, the energy itself has no physical existence, but yet is there in the wine and bread, capable of exerting an influence on the eaters of the bread and drinkers of the wine,so as to bring them closer to the understanding of Jesus by literally taking the spiritual force of Christ into their bodies and souls. Remembering that this was facilitated by the drawing of a sign that was associated with the powers of Jesus over the foodstuffs. So, can you do the same?

There was a time when I was involved with a group of witchcraft believers and as such I used a number of techniques that they did. I was encouraged to buy a crystal (a singular point of quartz on a necklace) and to use it to send energy to various objects. This I did, but trying to be a good laugh at the pub where I drank all the time, I used the crystal to change the properties of alcoholic drinks. I would take a concept that I was familiar with (whiskey), and use an altered state of consciousness, meditation and visualization, to focus on the colour of whiskey, the flavor and the sensation when whiskey is drunk and then directed that concept down my arm and into the beers that my friends were drinking. I visualized the golden whiskey energy pouring down the point of the stone and deeper and deeper into the beers, in my minds eye, coloring the whole beer with the apparently tangible whiskey energy. On drinking the beers, my friends (being disbelievers in the occult) where surprised to sense the flavor and burning down the throat that whiskey gives and to feel more drunken than they would if they were on beer alone.

So, what had I done here? Simply the same formula that the priest in the Church did. So, that shows that one can bless beer, wine and any drink, one can bless foods that people are going to eat, one can put the "energy" in physical objects and anyone who touches it will then get a shot of the energy and so on. To what extent that can create changes in the human mechanism that one can achieve remains down to your own experiment and speculation. However the results obtained from the whiskey experiment were so powerful and profound it does make us want to speculate further and further, but that would be going against the scientific line of investigation and we would fall prey to developing beliefs in things that are not necessarily real. We have, even in the light of such evidence, to always be skeptical of our own experiences.

But lets say that there was another direction that we could take the exercise, lets say that the economy is in a state of crisis, and there is doom and gloom in th news every day. You know that right now the company that you work for is dong ok, but you fear that in three months time thee may be a catastrophe and you will need another job at that time. You know that you will have to go out looking for work, you know that you will have to go through the mill of smiling and being sweet to the recruitment consultants as well as the lovely people (lol) that will be first and second stage interviewing you and you don't like that at all.

So, being a secret occultist, you decide that you will try and increase the probability of certain things happening in your life, namely the acquisition of work when you need it. You decide to make a energy force, based on all the energies of success and achievement, the feeling of getting a new job and the happiness that you will gave once you realize that the right job is going to come your way. You decide that just believing that it will happen if you do a ritual would be balderdash (but using a combination of occult techniques and down to earth straight forward job seeking activity would be ok wouldn't it?), but you still want to increase the chances of success in your life. So, you saturate your mind with images of success, you read books and watch films about business success, about young and struggling people bringing themselves up from the gutter to a life of happiness and joy. You don't do this just to cheer yourself up, but to learn the energies of success in the workplace. You take time over this and get to create a spirit that you associate with the energies of success. In occult terms, this might be called a servitor or servant, but there is no matter if this character appears to you wearing either angel wings or a business suit. Again you talk to it when in mediation, you learn to visualize it more and more strongly and start to have conversations with it, just for fun and play initially, but then after a time the being becomes more real to you. You create a sign or symbol that can be visualized or drawn easily with the finger over food or a drink and when no-one is looking you bless the food or drink with the sign of success, maybe visualizing the success at a job interview as you do so to focus the energy of the success into the foodstuffs that you are going to take. You choose to fortify this energy even more and take a small piece of wood of a type that you associate with the energies of money, wealth or stability (oak?) and using a hot skewer, you braise the images of the sign that you have created into the small piece of wood. Using the ritual of creating the circle and building the energy of the ritual by chanting the name that you have given this spiritual force, you at the crescendo, place the energy that you have raised into the item. Using a leather strap wear it around your neck or keep it in the pocket when you go for an interview (making sure that it can't be seen by the interviewer!). Then maybe you are pleasantly surprised when the employer gives you the job on the first day.... But that is purely psychological isn't it?

Ok, well maybe that example is purely psychological, and maybe there is another dimension to it. But what if after another 6 months at the job, you feel that one of your rivals is getting on your nerves and you want him out of the job. You know that after a few months it is Year End and your rival will have to do a presentation in front of the boss. Instead of creating a talisman for success, why not create one for nervousness, irritability, stress and failure?

Just think for a minute.... what ideas will you need and where will you get them? How will you create a symbol that appears to any onlooker to be a bit of folk art and nothing malevolent at all? How will you give it to him and what will you do to make sure that the energy that is personalized to him? During the ritual itself, what ideas would you use to protect yourself from the energies of failure entering into you? Will you add another aspect to your psychic attack by sending your cat spirit to him to give him bad dreams? Use your creativity! Magick is a creative and personal art after all, most of your "knowledge" will be through experience rather than repeating formula.

Again I say it, that magick is not something to be relied upon 100% nor its it to be used 100% all the time for these purposes otherwise you run the risk of becoming an addict to psychic stuff as well as loosing your marbles, but once in a while it can be fun to watch an adversary do badly at something. . . .

Another way that this "energy" can be used is as a weapon of sorts. There was a time when I had the great misfortune to know a character who also had occult beliefs, he spent much of his time upsetting me and deliberately being a bit of a pain. I hated him. One day at noon in a public location he stared one of his unpleasant an nonsensical arguments with me. I did successfully counter his argument and he left. I watched him walking away and suddenly I could not stand having the quantity of resentment, bitterness and anger in me against him any longer, it felt like my whole aura was full of spiritual excrement that was irritating every part of my being. As I watched him going away, I focused the negativity on the back of his neck and let all the anger out in one moment, without saying a word. I felt the sensation of the spiritual negativity leaving the aura as if it had been fired from a slingshot from my feet, through my upper body and out of my head and then along my line of sight to him. It felt like a mass of muddy fluid had been chucked out of my aura and I felt immediate emotional release. But my adversary, at that very moment staggered sideways as if someone had rather violently pushed him at the shoulder. I find it interesting in retrospect that after that very moment he changed his tactics with me and stopped trying to wind me up in the same way instead he used a certain type of arrogance combined with the occasional pleasantry which had the effect of diffusing the resentment in me to the point whereby I could not build up that same quantity of resentment against him, and therefore I could not attack him that way. It is possible that he realized what I was doing and as such chose a means of trying to diffuse the method that I could attack him with. I am not sure if I can actually do this at will, but it is more likely that I can only do this when I have that quantity of anger, violence and resentment deep in me. So if I wanted to attack someone again, I would have to keep clear of them (so that they can't choose to be nice to me) and master techniques of building up what can only be described as evil energy and intentions inside me prior to letting them out. But this also runs psychological risks that few people should consider. Whether the old medieval myth that if I was to have walked over water, I would have lost the power to attack has any truth to it, as Dion Fortune suggested, I have not given that a sufficient investigation to be able to say either way.

The mystery of the creation of magickal signs and symbols.

When we consider the idea of magickal symbols, you can react in a number of ways, one is that of Devil or demon theory whereby you feel that all signs themselves are somehow evil, and another can be that you must be mad to even consider the theory that symbology is somehow useful, another could be that you have to follow a tradition otherwise bad luck befalls you and so on. The list can be endless, but realistically, magickal symbols are merely something that you as an occultist use to focus your mind on a specific energy, mood, personality and the like. You can take them from tradition, you can take them form anti traditions and make your own up, it really matters not one fig where you get them from. It also matters not one fig whether you have made them yourself at home or whether they are part of an established construct. What matters is that they are simple enough to be able to be visualized or drawn in the air with a finger, specific enough to not be confuse with anything else, and descriptive enough to cover the meanings that you ascribe to them.

In the Chaos magick school of thought, magickal symbols are often created from the letters of a word or sentence. You write down the desire, cross off all the repeated letters and then scramble them in any way that you see fit. You then use the word thus formed from the letters as the mantra, and then create an abstract pastern simplified from the letters that you use as the object of meditation. This way you are using the visual and visualization senses, and the tactile senses of the creation of the symbol and the sense of sound and hearing through the chanting. Also the activity of chanting the same thing over and over can help to bring about a meditative trance.

The finished symbol can be drawn over a triangle (spirit trap) in a ritual circle to help to invoke the spiritual force of that symbol. It can be drawn over food and drink in the manner of the Eucharist, it can be visualized as the source code or DNA that a spirit that you wish to create can grow out of, or it can be the body of a spiritual force that you send out to do your bidding. Again use your creativity and have fun!

The main thing to do is to make sure that you have fully learned the ramifications of the sign, loaded it with meanings, the energies, the way that the spiritual energy is to have its effect.

(But lets think about how this same idea is used in the "real" world. A big company wants you to buy their products, thy create a suitably visually stunning TV commercial to grab your attention and to build interest in (I would argue) the similar manner as a ritual occultist building up the "energy" of a spiritual force in the circle. Then they focus your senses on the sound of an audible logo as well as physical representations of the product that they are trying to sell, as well as the symbol or spirit of the product. These averting methods are so powerful that they enter into the popular culture and then people start to play games with the words that they have heard and seen. Maybe the moment you hear the words "Hmmm Danone" you automatically visualize the probiotic drink? But occult methods seem to work on another level, something that is subconscious and deeper, or maybe to do with the aura. Who knows and to a certain degree, who cares? Play with it until you get somewhere and take it from there!).

Spiritualism

Some supernaturalist believe that they receive assistance from guides or some other entity, but when questioned as to how they know stuff or what they are picking up, they cannot answer you. You often get woolly and strange responses such as "try to think outwardly", "make contact with Spirit", "Reach out within and though the here and now to the place beyond" and often these strange and nonsensical statements are occasioned by a strange circular hand waving behavior that suggests that the spiritualist at the time that you are asking them does not actually know the meanings of the words that they are using and, at best, is struggling to find the right words to communicate the concepts to you, concepts that they probably don't understand themselves. So maybe it is not the fact that spirit contact happens or that spiritualists exist, but the fact that spiritualists don't know what the hell they are on about that makes the whole subject of the supernatural seem like such a load of hogwash to so many people. If for instance I became a plumber, and I decided to try and explain to a trainee what I was doing, I would have to explain the concepts the physics behind what I was playing at, the components that I needed for the job and the like. However spiritualists don't seem to be able to do this. And I would say that the more that you play with the states of mind, you may also be unable to explain the full states of mind that you are entering into. Describing something that is unusual, such as a different or abnormal state of consciousness, can be tricky.

Alphonse Louis Constant writing under the name Elephias Levi, in his book Transcendental Magic, stated that spirits spoke though the "transluicid, that is the imagination", so a concept that he was trying to explain would be that things that suddenly come into the mind of the ritualist or medium, have some kind of specific meaning. However one would have to be able to rule out any extraneous variables that might be causing those extra phenomena to come into the mind of the magician, if this model of the world has any truth in it you will have to be able to work out the precise texture of the emotion, the precise mood that you wee experiencing and the quality of the visualization that suddenly and unexpectedly appeared to the mind, and then to be able to work out whether that could have come from an external source rather than a physical / psychological one that was explicable. People also speak of Clairaudence and hearing the words of the spirits. Constant also spoke of this phenomena, he said that a spiritual force cannot create a voice, as it has no organs with which to vibrate the air to make sound "for how is a shadow to speak?" (read the chapter on Necromancy). In one of my many ritual activities, I did invoke into the circle a spiritual force that did essentially speak to me, but the sensation was rather strange, it was as if a bolt of lighting suddenly erupted from the spiritual being and struck my head and the meanings of words, but without sound, communicated to my consciousness at the same rate as if a person was speaking them to me. I "heard" the words of the Spirit deep inside my own head. A very interesting experience to say the least, and not the smallest bit frightening.

A theory of mine is that so many modern pagans and occultists focus the attention of their students or pupils on the concepts of ritual so much because they don't actually know what the hell they are doing when they do anything supernatural, and they are so terrified of the supernatural that they fall prey to superstitious behavior, namely believing in the ritual and not the components needed for success. This is probably the same as with mediumship and spiritualism. Not surprising as it is hard to explain what I mean when I am trying to describe the "emotion" of being in a state of theta meditation brought about my by mind machine brain wave entrainment device. For the moment lets forget about the Ouija board, and leave that for another section of this essay. For the moment lets just focus on the idea of spiritual contact.

When I was about the age of 4 and saw a lady in period costume waking between the closet and the door of my bedroom, (an experience that shaped my life forever), she was see though and vanished when she reached the location of door. However I still cannot say what it was that brought the experience about. How shall I therefore explain how to actually receive and make contact with spiritual entities?

It seems that there is some kind of very specific psychological muck up that one has to deliberately create in order to make and establish some kind of spiritual contact with an apparently disembodied entity. For the moment lets not worry about whether the spiritual force really is your dear darling grandmother or whatever and just try and describe what one needs to do to give this activity a go. During my history I have had some kinds of altered state experiences that were caused by allergies and nutritional problems. They did give me some interesting hallucinations such as the house being infested by cats. And seeing other things that "weren't there" (but might have been!). I became rather skilled at seeing small flashes of light that went between my fingers when I performed certain mantras that I devised for myself. But these mantras were designed by me to give me what I can only term are "spiritual sensations" and were part and parcel of the state of the development of a belief in God. (Which as I have pointed out is by no means proof of the existence or non existence of God). The mantra that I used was simply "I am ascending slowly to reach God" which I recited to myself slowly and silently over and over again. I tried to focus on the idea and presence of God, the sense of there being something caring and loving above me, and to "open the crown chakra" the energy center at the top of the head, through visualizing light emanating from the top of my head, and a beam of light descending from heaven to my head and into my body. I could then hold my hands up to before my eyes and then see sparks as bright as little electrical sparks passing between my fingers (With a bit of practice you too can do the same). The more that I practiced that exercise the more that I was able to increase the quantity of the effect that I had. With time I was able to get images and inspiration coming through. But I still could not safely say that what I was experiencing was coming from any direct form of spiritual force. And to be honest, if I apply any reasoning to what I actually experience then I still cannot say with 100% certainty that what I am receiving is real spiritual forces anyway. After a time, and with practice and perseverance, I did notice that just as Constant said in Transcendental Magic, that the eyeballs do have a tendency and desire to rotate upward and inward as the level of spiritual ecstasy becomes more and more intense. However, Constant suggested that this was due to the nervous system becoming intoxicated by the astral light, a spiritual force that he believed was responsible for the various effects that occurred in magickal activities. Whether this force actually exists or not is neither here nor there, but one can say that under certain conditions it does seem to have a level of existence. One thing that I did notice that Constant wrote about was something that did happen to me, he said that as the eyeballs rotate inward, the ecstatic (in this example, myself) should be experiencing visions from within, something coming through in the translucid, the imagination. I could not actually experience visions this way without actually asking the "spiritual forces" to give them to me, I would either have to go looking, namely perform some kind of remote viewing exercise (as mentioned in the section on astral projection), or would have to speak to these spiritual forces and then invite them to give me some kind of insight or experience to demonstrate their existence to me and to pass on any messages. When in this particular state, the visions would eventually come though in the form of glimpses of something that was then to happen or was somehow in accordance with the energies of what I was asking about. It was however a little too vague top be considered to be primary data or a 100% reliable source of information. This could well be the type of experience that Constant was talking about in Transcendental magick, the spirits speaking to the magician though the translucid. With further practice I could experience more and have a more in depth communion with apparently divine beings.

But, what if this experience can be expanded? What if one could actually use the same state of spiritual euphoria to experience the presence of beings, people, shades of the dead and other spiritual forces that people believe exist these days? Now this is where it gets difficult to explain, one of the many reasons that people in the occult community probably avoid the discussion of the precise mechanisms of how they do this is by its very nature difficult to define the feelings that one gets. But I can try and explain this in some kind of theoretical framework. Lets say for instance that you spent months or years purely practicing the development of this state of spiritual ecstasy, principally for fun and for pleasure, and then with the passage of time, you gained much more skill at doing the same thing, and the experience grew more and more intense and you would, when in that meditative state, trying to sense your soul being lifted up out of the crown of your head, and this powerful sensation get more and more real. Even, maybe to the point whereby you can block out the sounds of the traffic passing by the house and the sound of the TV on in the next room. By definition this would be a temporary state of insanity, an abnormality of the mind and possibly brain chemistry and activity too, but from your point, the point of the meditator, you are having a wonderful time sensing the presence of what appears to be divine and spiritual energy. The more that you play with this technique, the more that you get strange sensations, voices in the room with you, sounds, impressions and flashes of visions, then more time passes and you seem to see, or sense the presence of beings that you can describe with greater and greater detail. Over time you begin to realize that you can sometimes sense these presences when you are awake and going about your normal day to day life, you have become to all intents and purposes, a medium. But, how long can this take? Possibly years. If it takes so long to develop this state of being why would I bother with it? Well, I guess that is up to you, but there is no aspect of the supernatural that can be gained and no experience that can be received overnight. Just because you buy books from certain bookstores does not mean to say that you can suddenly give yourself the title of Magician. But, if there was a certain degree of pleasure that one can get from being in the state of spiritual ecstasy by the method as I have defined above, and it makes you calm and seems to give you a feeling that you are part of something greater, then there is no harm in it anyway, so why not only give it a go, but not to deliberately get results, but just for fun, enjoyment and if anything else comes from it then you will have an extra added benefit.

But, are there any extra aspects that one needs to go through to make the spiritualism exercise work better? Well, kinda, but for me to explain that I will have to revert back to being a bit wishy washy. When I was taking my notes and practicing with the technique outlined above, I would describe the changes in self perception that occurred during the meditations in a number of different ways. Firstly I would say that before the exercise, it seemed that my consciousness was between my eyes, a a little set back in my head, just like any other person, and with the increases in the state of mind, I would sense that my whole being and body somehow seemed larger, and that "I" was taking up larger cloud like shape over and above my head, I would attempt to shift the way that I sensed the world around, so that instead of trying to sense things of a physical nature that one does when one is performing mundane day to day exercises, I tried to focus the attention on more ethereal concepts, like convection currents in the room, other things that I could only just about feel but could not see under normal circumstances and definitely not with my eyes half open, I then progressed from that and tried to sense anytime else that was not of a standard physical nature and then to try in an almost paranoid way, to sense everything that was happening around me at once, the sounds made by the house expanding and contracting with temperature, the 50Hz buzz of the electrical cables in the property etc., and then to try and sense things that were of a higher nature even than that, my self and personal perception was being "opened" to experience what can only be classed as higher energies, temporarily developed the belief that there were entities around me that I built up in my imagination, and that I was trying to sense them, but from time to time another entity that I had not previously conceived of would appear to my apparently spiritual senses. Just as you can sometimes feel the emotions coming from a friend when you are in conversation with them, I would be able to feel the emotions, state of mind, and aspects of the personality of the dis-incarnate being possessed, maybe a businessman, a librarian, a person who traditionally wore colour such as brown and green when he was alive, a person who had hatred directed at certain individuals. All kinds of details would come though, many of them I would write down and then would find that a certain high percentage of the details that I received were somehow "accurate" to an individual associated with a person or place that I was near. People came to me for readings and all I did was to say what I saw and to be honest I was scared rigid with the similarities that seemed to occur in the reading situations (just because I am a professional supernaturalist doesn't mean to say that I don't get freaked out by what I do!).

So, you may think, why am I telling you all this stuff? Simply because I have sufficient trust and confidence that each and every person if they apply enough dedication, has the ability to develop the same "gifts" that I have done in the past. What you develop, why you develop them and how you do it is entirely up to you. I would say that if you wished to try supernatural activity for yourself, it would take you many months and years to be able to get some kind of results. And you don't have to be members of any religion that has supernatural beliefs to do so! (studies into Neuro-plasticity suggest that after 3 months or more of practicing any activity every day will actually change the structure of the brain to accommodate the skill in question. On top of that, the more minutes that you devote to the self training, the better the brain grows. Something to take into consideration when practicing!)

Ouija

No essay on the supernatural that has an occult edge to it can really be complete without a mention of the Ouija Board. I have seen good atheists shivering with fear when there is mention of the Ouija device. I have heard "stories" of people dying under its influence and have had Christan friends who don't "believe in such things" avoiding like the plague a object that is nothing more or less that a glorified game board with numbers and letters printed on it by an ink jet printer. The quantity of fear and apprehension that these devises create is well disproportional to the device itself and what can be achieved with it. I have never in my whole life seen with my physical eye, a demon with scaly skin breathing fire come out of a Ouija device. I have never noticed anything frightening from these devices at all. Remember that the Ouija is a game, noting more, its name is a trade mark and not anything supernatural. The word was not intended to be the words in French and German for yes, but was in fact supposed to be an Egyptian word for Good Luck, which it isn't! It is a device and nothing more, no it doesn't open up a doorway to hell and doesn't have the power to posses the minds of its users.

Essentially, Ouija is not the proper name for these devices, they are part of a family of items that are called "talking boards", but for the sake of convenience I will carry on calling the device the Ouija.

Indeed there is no evidence that the messages that come from the Ouija are in fact anything more than psychological, however as I have already pointed out there is little that can be proved pro or against the idea that these mechanisms can be or cannot be used to have some conversations with spiritual entities, as even the spiritual entities themselves, even by the experience of an occultist, cannot be 100% proven. You as a user of Ouija or any other from of divination device need to be aware that without the quantity of disbelief after the event of using Ouija or other toys, have the capacity to loose your marbles completely. I have seen women trying to contact their dead boyfriends and crying when the glass moved from letter to letter spelling out a message of his pain and discomfort in the soul of the boyfriend, and then developing a desire to go and "join" him, when the message was much more likely due to the strange mentality of the people who were present there, that one of the other séance sitters was playing with the poor girls mind through deliberately moving the glass. It is much better to experiment with Ouija devices at home and alone or with very very trustworthy friends, but with sufficient ability to develop disbelief after the event so as to save your mentality. However they take a lot of time to practice with to get the planchette or upturned whiskey tumbler to move apparently of its own free will, definitely many weeks. In each case you have to be prepared to take notes after the event, working with other people can add too many spurious factors into the mix and as such can make the whole experience rather difficult to ascertain where you are actually getting the information from. However, Ouija sessions are downright great fun and there should be nothing in heaven or hell that should dissuade you from using them and just enjoying yourself.

Ouija sessions in groups are a great way to bring people together and have a social time, an event that is there just for fun and entertainment, and you should have sufficient ability to make sure that you can see the event as for fun and not trying to unravel the secret mysteries of the universe. For of the message indicator, (planchette) spells out message that a particular individual has an evil spirit around them, and their temperament and mentality is sufficiently weakened or affected by neurosis and other unpleasant psychological combinations of states of mind, to actually take the Ouija's words of it and not the advice of another saner human being, then that person might end up in all sorts of scrapes and problems. Remember that the Ouija is not an evil thing, but the mentality of the user can be very easily affected by what comes from the board itself. If the user is of the right (or should I say "wrong") disposition, he or she might have something perfectly ordinary happen in his house, such as discovering that the draw in the kitchen is a bit wonky, and then to suggest that it was the doing of an evil spiritual force when in fact it was his or her own lack of due care and diligence with household maintenance that was to blame. The user might start to jump to conclusions about each and every bad happening that occurs in his or her life and will then pay an alleged professional magician many thousands of dollars to have the "curse of the Evil spirit" removed. The fake magician will then be more than happy to corroborate the pathogenic beliefs that the user has experienced, thus making the users mentality more and more unsteady and will then charge hundreds and thousands more dollars, each time assuring the user that he or she will get 100% results each time, eventually leaving the user penniless and in a need of psychiatric hospitalization.

This is the greatest abuse of the title of Magician, (spiritualist, Witch and many others) that can ever happen. I have in my earliest days of becoming a professional diviner been sought out by a lady who was being driven into poverty by an alleged miracle worker who called himself "Tel". This "Tel" was a very skilled conman. He cultivated the terror of the supernatural in the mind of his victim, he persuaded her that he was her friend and that all other forms of magick, witchcraft and occultism (funnily enough, not his own!) was evil and the work of a very real Devil, she spent hundreds of thousands of pounds to him, after all, he was a "high magician", or at least so that is what he said. The lady in question was so terrified of the unpleasantness of her life, that she invested all her belief into him. Until I had the ability to show her how to actually get out of her life problems using normal means and not using him. I taught her in a letter, that "Tel" was a false magician and a false friend, and that he was exploiting her. After she had received the letter, I received a short telephone message from her, it was just two words, "Thank You". I was just 17 at the time that I did this social miracle and freed my client from psychological and financial bondage.

I suppose that the reason that I am telling you this story primarily to point out to you that the biggest evils do not lie in the supernatural or the occult, but in the minds and actions of humans and as such you have to be on your guard and skeptical of anyone who either claims to be able to 100% reliably change the workings of the world, and even more so with people who actually believe that they can! These people are a major social, financial and psychological danger to all that they come across. If these people are not out for your money, then they are out to promote their own political or religious ideology or to get pleasure from your humiliation and failure. People who speak openly and passionately against the Ouija or any other tool of divination, or indeed the occult are essentially of this pathogenic type, either terrified in a superstitious way of something that cannot and will not affect them in any real way, or attempting to fortify the strange beliefs that surround their own religion, politics or ways of getting money. They are using a sort of brainwashing that is out in the open and not restricted to the practices of "official" cults. You are going to have to learn to disbelieve them if you are gong to play around with Ouija or any other form of device for the contact with supernatural entities or beings. If attempting to have an open conversation or debate with these people, you may find that it is merely a way that they can use to try and attack you by argumentation and not by any real evidence. You will probably find the experience difficult as there is none so deaf as those that won't hear. Their methods will be superficial, and will not under any circumstances take into account the full ramifications of the argument, instead they tease out at small fragments of information, and use them as fuel for the attack rather than looking at the whole picture. In getting into the occult you are opening yourself up to a massive international debate of extreme political and social proportions. It might be wise to resign from the debiting society.

But how should you use a talking board or Ouija? Again, experiment, play about and have fun with it, if you want to do some fun ritual first and then make it seem more magical and spiritual then by all means go for it, but for the board itself, again it takes many weeks and diligent practice to get any useful results at all. Start by placing the fingers on the planchette message indicator thing, with the elbows above an not resting on the table, relax. If you have already developed the ability to create and develop the sensation of being in spiritual ecstasy then by all means give that a go. Just like a performer in an orchestra, an actor or anyone else that matter you may wish to do some warming up exercises. Some call this warming up the board, but I feel that you are just loosening any tension in the fingers and arms that might inhibit the movement of the message indicator. Essentially make the planchette (deliberately!) move around the board in a seemingly random manner, this will increase the circulation of the blood to the finger and arm muscles and make you feel more supple and receptive. Initially you may well just be thinking that the whole thing is psychological anyway and as such you just move the pointer around to places where it just feels right, and use a tape recorder, wav or other digital voice recorder to record the gibberish that comes from the pointer spelling out messages. With more practice (after a few days or weeks), start to cultivate a new concept, choose to believe for the purposes of the exercise, that the planchette is moving of its own accord and that your hands are not being influenced by your own mind. To be able to convince yourself of this in any meaningful way will take a bit more time, but as you are practicing and I hope just dong this for fun, you don't have to obsess about the messages that come out of the Ouija. Time passes still further and with subsequent experiments that the planchette seems to move of its own accord and you are able to observe the messages that come from it.

Ask the questions of the Ouija out loud and then spell out to the voice recorder what actually the board spelled out for you, which symbols it pointed to and what that means in practice. Naturally after each session, take notes first of what you feel happened and then listen to the recording, you may detect some extraneous variables in the sound recording that you had forgotten about. With the passage of time and if you wish to turn Ouija into a specific skill set for you to use in your occult exploration, you may wish to perform the circle casting and then invoke a spiritual force that you had previously created or developed a relationship with in any other way and get that force to answer questions placed to it via the Ouija. Give the spiritual force control over your arms and hands. Tell the spiritual force to use your eyes to be able to locate the position of the letters, numbers and words on the board. Just see what happens and above all have fun.

If you are to see experimentation with the Ouija device as being the development of a skill, think to yourself, did the way that I ask questions affect the outcome? Did the food that I have been eating over the past few days or the quantity and quality of sleep that I have had recently affect the mood that I needed to enter into to get the results that I had? If you invited a spiritual being to come and help you and to communicate with you, were the signs an ideas that you used to invoke the spiritual entity sufficiently descriptive? Did I chant for long enough to bring the right quantity of presence to the circle? Was the circle visualized with sufficient force to make it seem and feel safe? Would it have worked better if a different colour alter cloth been used? Have I been doing enough meditation recently to train my mind up to the right level make the whole experience work to my benefit?

If you have been using symbology from your very own collection of symbols on your very own tree of life, were the colors and symbols more associated with what you felt were right for the angelic world or the demon world? Did the "results" reflect that? What else could you have done to increase the precision that you selected the nature of the spiritual entity that you summoned? This is the type and quality of questions that you need to ask yourself on the successful completion of the exercise and naturally it is the type of quality of questions that you need to ask yourself. If you are to see your own investigation into the world of magick as being scientific, make a study of yourself and all that you do! Make detailed notes and revisit them from time to time, that way you can assess your process and see how well you have done, which conclusions you have reached, whether it is actually worthwhile to keep those conclusions or are you concerned as to where those conclusions might take you long term? Keep in mind that practice makes progress. Also keep in mind that skepticism after the event is essential for the maintenance of your sanity.

Conclusion.

In this short essay, we have looked at many aspects of the supernatural and the way that individuals, any individuals, can experiment and make up what they see fit. I have kept the argument against the development of belief as a result of supernatural experience and I feel have kept the case for that quite plain. The main evil is not in the occult itself, but in the world of men and how people use supernatural ideas to control other people. After all, we are not dealing with the physical sciences here, we cannot say with 100% certainty anything about the way that the hidden world works but we can look at certain aspects of what we do, work out what results if any, were achieved and take note of the experiences.

The system magick of the Kaballa, Golden Dawn and other structured theological worlds con us into believing that there is structure to the world of the supernatural, spiritualism has lulled us into a false sense of security about the other world and life after death, Wicca has laid down rules for the operation of magick, but with no real evidence to back it up leaving only superstitious fear, ignorance about magickal activity and a terror of experimentation and the ability of certain individuals to use this fear to their advantage. Organized religion as told us that everything that is not of that religion is Evil, despite the evils of misunderstanding of the members of those religions. Authors such of a certain genre have done a power of good that marketing benefits can do to the supernatural industries as a direct result of advancing the culture of the industry, but have done all the harm in the world for the many people who give away their livelihood and self control to the fake and fraudulent readers and magicians who exploit so many people. Even freestyle magick, has started to coalesce out of the chaos into a system that takes for itself a structure and a system, incantations, signs and spells. The very word "magick" has been adjusted and adapted for people all over the world to the very point whereby it has lost all of its meaning. Belief and lack of reasoning has become King and ruler over an increasingly more powerless species of beings called Humans. It is truly time for humanity to get back to being able to experiment with and explore the supernatural nature of nature itself, and to do so without any fear of blasphemy against any religion or fear of crossing any deity. It is also truly time for humankind to realize that the words used in the English language are there for a purpose, to spread understandings and meaning and not to be abused.

If you are after self development, then get some group therapy, if you are after assertiveness then go on an assertiveness course, if you need religion, then get some, if you want to use visualization for the purposes of doing well in business, then read a motivational book, but magick, by its very name must be separate and different in terms of a set of ideas and methodologies, separate goals than the other aspects of human life as mentioned in this paragraph.

What is the point of you doing any magick or supernatural stuff? Well I am going to have to leave that for you to answer for yourself. Many people will just read this essay, think is is bad, evil, satanic and whatever they want if it disagrees with their world view, and then just discard it without having thought for a moment about the real reason that it was written and the power and autonomy that it was written to give. Others will think that they would like to entertain the ideas present in these pages but will decide to give up the practice of magickal activities in exchange for just gong out and having fun, whatever floats your boat. I am not here to tell you what to do. I would say that magick has given me the freedom to help get other people out of psychological and financial domination by other alleged occultists and has allowed me to try and use my perception and skill to help others, none of which has proven negative in any way whatsoever. I have also gained a lot of pleasure from the spiritual states of mind that I have been in an have received a few fun scares in my time too. It has all been worthwhile. All the time that I have spent in mediation and prayer has worked out a treat. Also the activities that I have done that have created results ("real" or apparent) in other peoples lives have had a very real impact on the wellbeing and happiness of the subjects. I have not taken away anyones free will power, I have been a facilitator in re-establishing power and the focus of control in the lives of all that I have touched during my occult career. In subsequent essays I will elaborate in greater depth and focus more on healing and divination. Remember this though, the most well quoted definition of magick "magick is the science and art of change in accordance with the will" was written by Alistair Crowley. This was not to describe or define the performance of miraculous or supernatural activities in accordance with the will, but as a pseudo scientific attitude to life as part and parcel of the cult that he was trying to create. Further evidence of the fact that his definition of magick was not to do with supernatural activity was later in Crowleys "Magick in Theory and Practice" whereby he defines magick as being "to be and to do" and therefore nothing remotely to do with supernatural activity. He also stated that the purpose of "magick' as defined by him was to become prosperous. However he did not define even remotely how the pentagrams, rituals and other forms of prattling around with a pointy hat on the head could help you to get prosperous. Other critics have suggested that magick as defined by Crowley was to generate a wide variety of religious experiences. A definition that he didn't use at all, despite the multitude of allusions to "inflame thyself with prayer" as to be the means to generate supernatural results from religious/occult ritual.

Crowley's legacy was to create a state of self importance to many would be magicians, pompous teenage philosophers and neurotic pagan types through the repetition of the phrase and absorption of the idea that "Magick is the Science and Art of change in accordance with the will", without even the remotest thought for the depth of meaning of the words "art" or "science" and what one has to do to be able to define oneself as either an artist or scientist, thus preventing intellectual growth and maturation in the occult practitioners of this time and halting any intelligent research be it formalized and institutionalized, or informal into the supernatural. (If you were to take a piece of paper and a pen and write down all the different types of artists and scientists that there are, and then work out what the words actually mean, you will see how mundane, but meticulous one would have to be.)

Instead of any intelligent exploration in to the occult or supernatural for the purposes of creating real and measurable effects in the natural world, the occult community have accepted without question the superstitions of alternative therapies or religions (both new, traditional, orthodox and allegedly ancient) as being facts of the natural world. Instead of trying to fulfill the promises of magick (to heal diseases, affect the weather etc.), they water down the supernatural supermarket to the point of helping people to develop "spiritually" without defining what the heck they mean by "spiritual", primarily through avoiding any analysis as to the way that others have used the word. Many promise miracles, but surprisingly (LOL) do not perform any as it might affect their "karma". A interesting and useful escape clause for any inept !!! Become a magickian by all means, but make sure that you know the meanings of the words that you are using.

NOTES

NOTES

NOTES

www.ingramcontent.com/pod-product-compliance
Lightning Source LLC
Chambersburg PA
CBHW081600040426
42446CB00014B/3222